PIPER

EMMA CHICHESTER CLARK

To Laura

Text © 1995 Laura Cecil, Illustrations © 1995 by Emma Chichester Clark.
First published in Great Britain in 1995 by Jonathan Cape, London.
Revised edition first published in 2005 by Andersen Press Ltd. London.

This edition published in 2007 by agreement with Andersen Press by
Eerdmans Books for Young Readers
an imprint of Wm. B. Eerdmans Publishing Co.
2140 Oak Industrial Dr. N.E., Grand Rapids, Michigan 49505
P.O. Box 163, Cambridge CB3 9PU U.K.

www.eerdmans.com/youngreaders

Manufactured in Singapore

07 08 09 10 11   8 7 6 5 4 3 2 1

Library of Congress Cataloging-in-Publication Data
Chichester Clark, Emma.
Piper / written and illustrated by Emma Chichester Clark.
p. cm.
Summary: A young dog runs away from its cruel master, but finds
a new home after saving the life of an old woman.
ISBN: 978-0-8028-5314-1 (alk. paper)
[1. Dogs--Fiction.]   I. Title.
PZ7.C4328Pi 2007
[E]--dc22
2006008548

Text type set in Poppl-Pontifex
The illustrations were created in watercolor inks and colored crayons

Gayle Brown, Art Director
Matthew Van Zomeren, Graphic Designer

PIPER

EMMA CHICHESTER CLARK

Eerdmans Books for Young Readers

Grand Rapids, Michigan • Cambridge, U.K.

When Piper was a little puppy, his mother used to
say to him, "Always obey your master. Always
look both ways before you cross the street. And always
help anyone in danger."

Once Piper was old enough to leave home Mr. Jones, his new master, came to take him away. He was a strange, fierce looking man and Piper felt nervous.

"Don't worry," said Piper's mother comfortingly. "If you remember the three things I told you, you will be a good dog and I will always be proud of you."

Mr. Jones dragged Piper up a hill to the lonely crooked house where he lived.

"Tomorrow I want you to take care of the rabbits in my vegetable patch. Teach them a lesson they won't forget!" said Mr. Jones grimly.

I can easily obey that command, thought Piper.

Piper worked very hard. He took good care of the rabbits all day and by evening he had taught them to jump over him. They had a lovely time.

But Mr. Jones was furious. He came up behind
Piper and hit him with a big stick. "You stupid
disobedient dog!" he snarled. "You were supposed
to get rid of the rabbits! Stay in this shed until I
decide what to do with you."

He tied poor Piper up,
without any food.

But the rabbits didn't forget Piper. They visited
him every night and brought him their food. Piper
thought they were very kind, though he didn't
enjoy eating lettuce.

A week later Mr. Jones bought a new dog. It was a vicious creature with teeth like knives.

"Brutus will get rid of all the rabbits," said Mr. Jones. "And then he will teach you how to be a real dog!" Brutus growled at Piper and bared his sharp teeth. Piper was terrified.

That night Piper bit through the rope and escaped.

He ran and ran through dark woods.

He ran up and down steep hills.

And he plunged across a river.

At last he came to a big city. It was dark and noisy. The houses were like gray boxes. Everywhere cars and trucks hurried by. Piper looked both ways and tried to cross the street. But the traffic never stopped. He felt very small and alone.

Then Piper saw an old lady standing on the other side of the street. She called to him and he gave a friendly bark in return.

Suddenly she stepped out towards him into the street without looking! A car was about to run her over! Piper darted in front of her and stopped the car. But the old lady was so startled that she fell backwards onto the pavement. She lay there without moving.

Soon a crowd gathered and an ambulance arrived.
The ambulance men gently lifted the old lady onto a
stretcher and took her away.

Piper was miserable.
Nobody noticed him
sitting there, so he
crept away.

Piper had banged his leg on the car when
he saved the old lady. He limped sadly along
until he came to a park.

It began to rain. His leg hurt very much
when he walked so he hid under a bush.

As he drifted off to sleep, Piper dimly heard voices through the raindrops drumming on the trees.

Suddenly there was a loud shout
nearby. "I've found him!"

Piper felt himself being gently lifted up and wrapped in a warm blanket. Then he fell asleep. He did not understand that everyone had been looking for the brave dog who had saved the old lady's life.

When he woke up he was lying on a soft sofa with a bowl of delicious food in front of him. And there was the old lady smiling at him! "You are a hero," she said.

"I'd like you to live with me," said the old lady. "But first I have to put up signs to say that I have found you, in case your owner wants you back. If no one claims you after a week then you can stay."

FOUND

Black dog, v. thin,
long tail.
Owner please ring
352794
within seven days
if wanted.

Piper couldn't explain that he never wanted to
see his cruel owner again. Every day he waited
in case Mr. Jones called.

By the end of the week he was so tired he fell asleep by the telephone.

Suddenly it rang!

The old lady lifted the receiver and Piper heard Mr. Jones's grating voice:

"That black dog is mine, but you're welcome to him. He is such a coward he won't even chase a rabbit!"

"I should hope not, you horrible man," said the old lady in a shocked voice, and she put the receiver down with a bang.

"How lucky I am to have found you," she said.
"Now we can both look after each other."